Awesome

ANIMAL JOKES

for Kids!

BOB PHILLIPS

HARVEST HOUSE PUBLISHERS
Eugene, Oregon 97402

Cover by Terry Dugan Design, Minneapolis, Minnesota

AWESOME ANIMAL JOKES FOR KIDS
Copyright © 1998 by Bob Phillips
Published by Harvest House Publishers
Eugene, Oregon 97402

ISBN: 1-56507-791-1

Published in the United States of America.

98 99 00 01 02 03 / BC / 10 9 8 7 6 5 4 3

Contents

$$\boxed{1}$$

Daffy Dinosaurs

Why does a dinosaur have cracks between his toes?

To carry his library card.

First man: What's the difference between a lemon, a dinosaur, and a tube of glue?

Second man: I give up.

First man: You can squeeze a lemon, but you can't squeeze a dinosaur.

First man: What about the tube of glue?

Second man: That's where you get stuck.

Why don't more dinosaurs join the police force?

They can't hide behind billboards.

Why did the dinosaur walk on two legs?

To give the ants a chance.

Why is it dangerous to go into the jungle between two and four in the afternoon?

That's when dinosaurs are jumping out of palm trees!

Why does a dinosaur climb a tree?

To get in his nest!

What weighs two pounds, is gray, and flies?

A two-pound dinosaur bird!

Why do dinosaurs have long toenails on Friday?

Because their manicurist doesn't come until Saturday!

What did the man say when he saw the dinosaurs coming down the path wearing sunglasses?

Nothing! He didn't recognize them!

Why don't dinosaurs take ballet lessons?

They outgrew their leotards!

Why do dinosaurs have wrinkles in their knees?

They stayed in the swimming pool too long!

Why do dinosaurs climb trees?

There's nothing else to climb in the jungle!

How can you tell a male dinosaur from a female dinosaur?

Ask it a question. If he answers, it's a male; if she answers, it's a female.

Why did the dinosaur fall out of a palm tree?

A hippopotamus pushed him out!

Why do dinosaurs have flat feet?

They don't wear sneakers!

How can you tell if a dinosaur is visiting your house?

His tricycle will be parked outside.

Why did the dinosaur lie on his back in the water and stick his feet up?

So you could tell he wasn't a bar of soap!

Why do dinosaurs wear glasses?
*To make sure they don't step on other
  dinosaurs!*

What do you know when you see three
  dinosaurs walking down the street wearing
  pink sweatshirts?
*You need help. Whoever heard of three
  dinosaurs walking down the street wearing
  pink sweatshirts?*

What's red on the outside and green on the
  inside?
A dinosaur wearing red pajamas!

2

Kangaroo Crack-Ups

First kangaroo: Why did the little girl take hay to bed?

Second kangaroo: To feed her nightmare.

First kangaroo: Why did the rabbit go to the doctor?

Second kangaroo: Because he felt jumpy!

First kangaroo: What happened to the two bedbugs who fell in love?

Second kangaroo: They were married in the spring!

First kangaroo: Why can't you tell secrets on a farm?

Second kangaroo: Because the corn has ears, the potatoes have eyes, the grass whispers, and the horses carry tails.

First kangaroo: What did the Cinderella fish wear to the ball?

Second kangaroo: Glass flippers.

First kangaroo: What's smarter than a talking horse?

Second kangaroo: A spelling bee.

First kangaroo: What did the duck say when it laid a square egg?

Second kangaroo: Ouch!

First kangaroo: When is it socially correct to serve milk in a saucer?

Second kangaroo: When you're feeding the cat.

First kangaroo: How do you tell the difference between an elephant and a rhinoceros?
Second kangaroo: The elephant has a better memory.

First kangaroo: What does a frog say when it washes car windows?
Second kangaroo: Rub it, rub it, rub it.

First kangaroo: What has feathers and writes?
First kangaroo: A ballpoint hen.

First kangaroo: Which is the bossiest ant?
First kangaroo: Tyrant!

First kangaroo: What do moose do at a concert?
Second kangaroo: Make moosic.

First kangaroo: What do you call it when giraffes moving one way, get mixed up with giraffes moving another way?

Second kangaroo: A giraffic jam.

First kangaroo: If you were surrounded by 30 lions, 25 elephants, and 10 hippos, how would you get away from them?

Second kangaroo: Step off the merry-go-round.

First kangaroo: Which ant is an army officer?

Second kangaroo: Sergeant!

First kangaroo: What do monkeys eat for dessert?

Second kangaroo: Chocolate chimp cookies.

3

Aardvark
Knock-Knocks

First aardvark: Knock, knock.
Second aardvark: Who's there?
First aardvark: Oscar.
Second aardvark: Oscar who?
First aardvark: Oscar for a date!

First aardvark: Knock, knock.
Second aardvark: Who's there?
First aardvark: Willie.
Second aardvark: Willie who?
First aardvark: Willie be home for dinner?

First aardvark: Knock, knock.
Second aardvark: Who's there?
First aardvark: Hans.
Second aardvark: Hans who?
First aardvark: Hans off the table!

First aardvark: Knock, knock.
Second aardvark: Who's there?
First aardvark: Isadore.
Second aardvark: Isadore who?
First aardvark: Isadore necessary?

First aardvark: Knock, knock.
Second aardvark: Who's there?
First aardvark: Raymond.
Second aardvark: Raymond who?
First aardvark: Raymond me to buy milk!

First aardvark: Knock, knock.
Second aardvark: Who's there?
First aardvark: Walter.

Second aardvark: Walter who?

First aardvark: Walter-wall carpeting!

First aardvark: Knock, knock.

Second aardvark: Who's there?

First aardvark: Martha.

Second aardvark: Martha who?

First aardvark: Martha right here and open the door!

First aardvark: Knock, knock.

Second aardvark: Who's there?

First aardvark: Althea.

Second aardvark: Althea who?

First aardvark: Althea later, alligator!

First aardvark: Knock, knock.

Second aardvark: Who's there?

First aardvark: Willa.

Second aardvark: Willa who?

First aardvark: Willa you go on a date with me?

First aardvark: Knock, knock.
Second aardvark: Who's there?
First aardvark: Henrietta.
Second aardvark: Henrietta who?
First aardvark: Henrietta the dessert.

First aardvark: Knock, knock.
Second aardvark: Who's there?
First aardvark: Jewel.
Second aardvark: Jewel who?
First aardvark: Jewel know when you
    open the door.

First aardvark: Knock, knock.
Second aardvark: Who's there?
First aardvark: Harriet.
Second aardvark: Harriet who?
First aardvark: Harriet up and open the door!

First aardvark: Knock, knock.
Second aardvark: Who's there?

First aardvark: Frank.
Second aardvark: Frank who?
First aardvark: Frank and beans.

First aardvark: Knock, knock.
Second aardvark: Who's there?
First aardvark: Ken.
Second aardvark: Ken who?
First aardvark: Ken you see me?

First aardvark: Knock, knock.
Second aardvark: Who's there?
First aardvark: Arnold.
Second aardvark: Arnold who?
First aardvark: Arnold you tired of all these knock-knock jokes?

First aardvark: Knock, knock.
Second aardvark: Who's there?
First aardvark: Lenny.
Second aardvark: Lenny who?
First aardvark: Lenny in—I'm cold out here!

First aardvark: Knock, knock.
Second aardvark: Who's there?
First aardvark: Randy.
Second aardvark: Randy who?
First aardvark: Randy four-minute mile!

First aardvark: Knock, knock.
Second aardvark: Who's there?
First aardvark: Chuck.
Second aardvark: Chuck who?
First aardvark: Chuck and see if the door is
  unlocked.

4

Caribou Crazies

First caribou: Did you hear the joke about the
rotten dinosaur eggs?

Second caribou: No.

First caribou: Two bad!

First caribou: Did you hear about the ten tons
of woolly mammoth hair that was stolen
from the wig-maker today?

Second caribou: No, I haven't.

First caribou: The police are now combing the
area.

First caribou: How do you stop a dinosaur from biting his nails?

Second caribou: I give up?

First caribou: Pull his foot out of his mouth.

First caribou: Ask me if I'm a rabbit.

Second caribou: Okay. Are you a rabbit?

First caribou: Yes, I'm a rabbit. Now ask me if I'm a caribou.

Second caribou: I'm game. Are you a caribou?

First caribou: No, silly. I told you I'm a rabbit.

First caribou: What kind of math do owls like?

Second caribou: Owlgebra.

First caribou: What kind of bears like to go out in the rain?

Second caribou: Drizzly bears.

First caribou: What do snake charmers wear around their necks?

Second caribou: Boaties.

First caribou: What do snakes learn in school?
Second caribou: Reading, writhing, and arith-
metic.

First caribou: What do you call a bee that
can't make up his mind?
Second caribou: A maybee!

First caribou: What well-known cartoon char-
acter do moths like a hole lot?
Second caribou: Mickey Moth!

First caribou: How can you make a tarantula
shake?
Second caribou: Run up behind it and say,
BOO!

First caribou: Which bug does amazing motor-
cycle stunts?

Second caribou: Evel Boll Weevil!

First caribou: Which bug gobbles up trash?
Second caribou: The litterbug!

First caribou: Where do cows go for lunch?
Second caribou: The calfeteria.

First caribou: What do you call two spiders
who just got married?

Second caribou: Newlywebs.

First caribou: What do you get when you
cross a frog with a can of soda?

Second caribou: Croak-a-Cola!

First caribou: Why does the giraffe have such
a long neck?

Second caribou: Because his head is so far
from his body!

5

Animal Freeway

How do you keep a dog from crossing the road?

You put him in a barking lot.

Why did the pigs cross the road with their laundry?

They wanted to do their hogwash.

Did you hear about the two kangaroos who crossed the road?

They jumped into each other's pouches and were never seen again.

Why did the one-handed gorilla cross the road?

To get to the secondhand shop.

What do you call a chicken that crosses the road without looking both ways?

Dead.

Why did the frogs cross the road?

To get a Croak-a-Cola.

Why did the rabbit cross the road?

To get to the hopping mall.

Why did the wasp cross the road?

It needed to go to the waspital.

Why did the hen go halfway across the road and stop?
She wanted to lay it on the line.

Why did the sheep cross the road?
He needed to go to the baabaa shop.

Why did the otter cross the road?
To get to the otter side.

Why did the elephant cross the road?
To pick up the squashed chicken.

Why did the sick rabbits cross the road?
They needed to go to the hopital.

What was the farmer doing on the other side of the road?
Catching all the chickens who crossed the road.

Why do skunks always argue when crossing the road?

'Cause they like to raise a stink.

Why did the turkey cross the road?

It was the chicken's day off.

Why did the chicken cross the road by the playground?

To get to the other slide.

Where do animals go when they lose their tails?

They go across the road to the retail shop.

Why did the duck cross the road?

Because the chicken retired and moved to Florida.

Why did the chicken cross the muddy road
and not come back?
*Because he didn't want to be a dirty double-
crosser!*

Why did the goose cross the road?
Because the light was green.

Why did the hen cross the street?
To see a man lay bricks.

Why did the cow cross the road?
To get to its fodder.

Did you hear the story about the peacock who
crossed the road?
It is really a colorful tail. . .

Why did the turtle cross the road?
To get to the shell station.

Why did the rooster cross the street?
To get to the other side.

6

Wallaby Wisecracks

First wallaby: What do you call a sleeping bull?

Second wallaby: I can't guess.

First wallaby: A bulldozer.

First wallaby: What do you call a cat who drinks lemonade?

Second wallaby: Beats me.

First wallaby: A sourpuss.

First wallaby: What is worse than a giraffe with a sore throat?

Second wallaby: I have no idea.
First wallaby: A centipede with blisters.

First wallaby: What goes "99, clump! 99, clump! 99, clump!"?
Second wallaby: You tell me.
First wallaby: A centipede with a wooden leg.

First wallaby: What does a dog make his clothes out of?
Second wallaby: I give up.
First wallaby: Mutterial.

First wallaby: Did you know that a grasshopper can jump four times its own length—and sometimes even more?
Second wallaby: Yeah, but once I saw a hornet lift a two-hundred-pound man one foot off the ground.

First wallaby: What kind of teeth can a deer buy for a dollar?
Second wallaby: Who knows?
First wallaby: Buck teeth.

First wallaby: What's worse than a hoarse horse?

Second wallaby: You've got me.

First wallaby: A chicken chicken.

First wallaby: Why did the farmer name his hog Ink?

Second wallaby: My mind is a blank.

First wallaby: Because he was always running out of his pen.

First wallaby: What has two heads, one tail, four legs on one side, and two legs on the other?

Second wallaby: That's a mystery.

First wallaby: A horse with a lady riding sidesaddle.

First wallaby: How does a skunk defend itself?

Second wallaby: I'm blank.

First wallaby: Instink.

First wallaby: How does a farmer take a sick
   pig to the hospital?
Second wallaby: I don't have the foggiest.
First wallaby: In a hambulance.

First wallaby: Why was the baby chicken
   thrown out of school?
Second wallaby: It's unknown to me.
First wallaby: It was caught peeping during a
   test.

First wallaby: What has 20 sharp teeth, a 90-
   foot tail, and scales all over it?
Second wallaby: I'm in the dark.
First wallaby: I don't know, but you'd better
   run if you see one!

First wallaby: What has an elephant's trunk,
   a giraffe's neck, a bird's beak, and a lion's
   head?
Second wallaby: Search me.
First wallaby: A zoo.

First wallaby: Why does a man who has just shaved look like a wild animal?

Second wallaby: You've got me guessing.

First wallaby: Because he has a bear face.

First wallaby: What did the leopard say when he finished the hot dog?

Second wallaby: I pass.

First wallaby: That hit the spot.

First wallaby: Ten cats were in a boat. One jumped out. How many were left?

Second wallaby: Nine.

First wallaby: Wrong. None were left. All the rest were copycats.

First wallaby: What animal has two humps and is found in Alaska?

Second wallaby: How should I know?

First wallaby: A lost camel.

First wallaby: What's all muddy and goes
around on Easter passing out eggs?

Second wallaby: I don't know.

First wallaby: The Easter Pig.

First wallaby: What is the best way to talk to
a hot dog?

Second wallaby: I have no clue.

First wallaby: Be frank.

7

Bobcat Buffoonery

What has three wings, three eyes, and two beaks?

A bird with spare parts.

What do you get when you cross a sheep dog and a bunch of roses?

A collieflower.

Who has eight guns and terrorizes the ocean?

Billy the Squid.

What lurks around the bottom of the sea and makes offers you can't refuse?

The Codfather.

Who snatched the baby octopus and held it for ransom?

Squidnappers.

What is black and white and has 16 wheels?

A zebra on roller skates.

What kind of doctor treats ducks?

A quack doctor.

Why did the chicken run away from home?

Because it felt cooped up.

What do you get if a pig studies karate?

A pork chop.

What do you call a bee with a low buzz?
A mumble bee.

Why did the elephant swallow a mothball?
To keep moths out of his trunk.

How do fish go into business?
They start on a small scale.

What do you get if you cross an elephant and a skunk?
A big stink.

What does a cat like to eat at breakfast time?
Mice Crispies.

Why do elephants lie in the sun a lot?
Because no one likes a white elephant.

Which bird is always out of breath?
A puffin.

What do you get if you cross a shark with a
parrot?
An animal that talks your head off.

What are white and furry and ride horses?
Polo bears.

Where would you find flying rabbits?
In the hare force.

What do you call a black sheep that's just
been sheared?
Bare, bare, black sheep.

What travels underground at 80 miles an
hour?
A mole on a motorbike.

What goes tick-tock woof, tick-tock woof?
A watchdog.

Where do cats like to go for vacations?
The Canary Islands.

8

How Fast Do Animals Move?

In the Air

Fly	5 mph
Bat	15 mph
Blue Jay	20 mph
Robin	30 mph
Owl	40 mph
Dragonfly	50 mph
Hummingbird	60 mph
Canvasback duck	70 mph
Golden eagle	120 mph
Duck hawk	180 mph

On the Land

Snake	1/10 mph
Turtle	2 mph

Man............................... 20 mph
Elephant .... 25 mph
Cat............................... 30 mph
Ostrich........................... 40 mph
Jack Rabbit .... 45 mph
Gazelle........................... 50 mph
Cheetah.......................... 70 mph

In the Water

Goldfish.......................... 4 mph
Man............................... 5 mph
Pike.............................. 6 mph
Whale .... 20 mph
Dolphin .... 25 mph
Barracuda .... 30 mph

9

Hairy Gorilla

What did they make Hairy Gorilla do when
he drew a line three blocks long at his
movie?

They made him erase it!

What do you have when you give a hairy
gorilla a piggyback ride?

A monkey on your back.

What would you get if you crossed a hairy
gorilla with a cockroach?

We don't know—but you'd better not step on it!

Why did the hairy gorilla keep falling out of
the tree?

Because he built his treehouse upside down!

If you were Hairy Gorilla's brother and he
had a baby boy, what would that make you?

A monkey's uncle!

Why did the hairy gorilla go on a diet?

So he could fit into his Volkswagen!

Why did the hairy gorilla take a sleeping pill
with a diet pill?

Because he wanted to take a light nap!

When do you give a hairy gorilla a going-
away present?
When you want him to go away!

What happened when the hairy gorilla took a
midnight stroll through New York City?
He got mugged.

What do you call the woman who marries a
hairy gorilla?
Mrs. Gorilla.

Why should you never hit a hairy gorilla
when he's down?
Because he might get up!

How do you stop a hairy gorilla from burping?
*Hold him over your shoulder, and pat him on
the back!*

How do you shake hands with a hairy gorilla?
Very carefully!

10

Octopus Knock-Knocks

First octopus: Knock, knock.
Second octopus: Who's there?
First octopus: Franz.
Second octopus: Franz who?
First octopus: Franz and Romans, coun-
   trymen lend me your ear.

First octopus: Knock, knock.
Second octopus: Who's there?
First octopus: Diane.
Second octopus: Diane who?
First octopus: Diane to meet you!

First octopus: Knock, knock.

Second octopus: Who's there?

First octopus: Orange.

Second octopus: Orange who?

First octopus: Orange you even going to open the door?

First octopus: Knock, knock.

Second octopus: Who's there?

First octopus: Cash.

Second octopus: Cash who?

First octopus: Cash me if you can!

First octopus: Knock, knock.

Second octopus: Who's there?

First octopus: Gus.

Second octopus: Gus who?

First octopus: Gus you don't want to play. . .

First octopus: Knock, knock.

Second octopus: Who's there?

First octopus: Hank.

Second octopus: Hank who?

First octopus: Hank you for opening the door.

First octopus: Knock, knock.

Second octopus: Who's there?

First octopus: Sherwood.

Second octopus: Sherwood who?

First octopus: Sherwood be nice if you opened the door.

First octopus: Knock, knock.

Second octopus: Who's there?

First octopus: Esau.

Second octopus: Esau who?

First octopus: E-sa-u looking out the window.

First octopus: Knock, knock.

Second octopus: Who's there?

First octopus: Yuri.

Second octopus: Yuri who?

First octopus: Yuri great person.

First octopus: Knock, knock.
Second octopus: Who's there?
First octopus: Juan.
Second octopus: Juan who?
First octopus: Juan to hear some more knock-knock jokes?

First octopus: Knock, knock.
Second octopus: Who's there?
First octopus: Louis.
Second octopus: Louis who?
First octopus: Louis'n up, don't be so uptight!

First octopus: Knock, knock.
Second octopus: Who's there.
First octopus: Cook.
Second octopus: Cook who?
First octopus: Cut the bird impressions, I want to come in!

First octopus: Knock, knock.
Second octopus: Who's there?
First octopus: Ezra.

Second octopus: Ezra who?
First octopus: Ezra a doctor in the house?

First octopus: Knock, knock.
Second octopus: Who's there?
First octopus: William.
Second octopus: William who?
First octopus: Williamind your own business!

First octopus: Knock, knock.
Second octopus: Who's there?
First octopus: Yoda.
Second octopus: Yoda who?
First octopus: Yoda le-hee-who!

First octopus: Knock, knock.
Second octopus: Who's there?
First octopus: Mikey.
Second octopus: Mikey who?
First octopus: Mikey won't fit in this lock!

First octopus: Knock, knock.
Second octopus: Who's there?
First octopus: Atlas.
Second octopus: Atlas who?
First octopus: Atlas you answered the door!

First octopus: Knock, knock.
Second octopus: Who's there?
First octopus: Noah.
Second octopus: Noah who?
First octopus: Noah one you know.

First octopus: Knock, knock.
Second octopus: Who's there?
First octopus: Isabella.
Second octopus: Isabella who?
First octopus: Isabella don't work—that's why I'm knocking.

First octopus: Knock, knock.
Second octopus: Who's there?
First octopus: Cain?
Second octopus: Cain who?
First octopus: Cain you come out to play?

First octopus: Knock, knock.
Second octopus: Who's there?
First octopus: Colleen.
Second octopus: Colleen who?
First octopus: Colleen up your room; it's
   a mess.

First octopus: Knock, knock.
Second octopus: Who's there?
First octopus: Neil.
Second octopus: Neil who?
First octopus: Neil and pray!

First octopus: Knock, knock.
Second octopus: Who's there?
First octopus: Ford.
Second octopus: Ford who?
First octopus: Ford he's a jolly good fellow.

First octopus: Knock, knock.
Second octopus: Who's there?

First octopus: Stalin.
Second octopus: Stalin who?
First octopus: Stalin for time!

First octopus: Knock, knock.
Second octopus: Who's there?
First octopus: Handel.
Second octopus: Handel who?
First octopus: Handel with care!

$$\boxed{11}$$

Elegant Elephants

What's the difference between a loaf of bread
  and an elephant?

*Well, if you don't know the difference, I'm
certainly not going to send you to the store
for a loaf of bread.*

Why can't elephants hitchhike?
They don't have thumbs!

Why do elephants roll down the hill?
Because they can't roll uphill very well!

How do you know when there's an elephant in your bathtub?
You can smell the onions on his breath.

Where do you find elephants?
It depends on where you leave them!

Why do elephants wear sneakers when jumping from tree to tree?
They don't want to slip and fall!

Why do elephants catch colds?
You would too if you ran around without any clothes on!

What do you find between elephants' toes?
Slow-running natives!

What's the worst part of eating elephants?
You have leftovers for weeks and weeks and weeks!

How do you greet a three-headed elephant?
Hello! Hello! Hello!

How do we know the age of elephants?
By going to their birthday parties!

Why did the elephant's tusks keep falling out?
*Who knows—maybe they'd have stayed in
   longer if he had used fluoride toothpaste!*

How did the elephant go on a diet?
It ate a cottage-cheese factory!

What does an elephant eat?
Just about anything it wants!

What do you do with a green elephant?
Wait until it ripens.

Do elephants make good house pets?
Only if they are housebroken!

12

Wisecackles

Why did the rooster crow before daybreak?

His cluck was fast.

What is another expression for chicken feed?

A poultry sum.

What's the best way to catch a chicken?

*Hide in the coop and make a noise like a
    bread crumb.*

What do you call an illiterate chicken?
A numb cluck.

What do you call a radical chicken?
A left-winger.

What do they call a chicken who keeps missing free throws in a basketball game?
A fowl-up.

What is the name of a chicken's holiday?
April Fowl's Day.

What musical instrument is associated with chickens?
Drumsticks.

What was the name of the famous chicken explorer?
Admiral Bird.

Why do chickens like George Washington?
Because he was the feather of our country.

What do they call a chicken who fails his test
in school?
A dumb cluck.

Why didn't the chickens go outside and play?
Because it was fowl weather outside.

What special day of the year honors roosters?
Feather's Day.

13

Ridiculous Raccoon Jokes

First raccoon: The woolly mammoths helped improve the neighborhood.

Second raccoon: How'd they do that?

First raccoon: They moved.

First raccoon: Did you ever try to tickle a mule?

Second raccoon: No. Why?

First raccoon: You'd get a big kick out of it!

60

First raccoon: I can imitate any bird.
Second raccoon: I think I can, too.
First raccoon: How about a homing pigeon?

First raccoon: Are you getting a new hairdo
for the party?
Second raccoon: No, I'm having a henna-do.
First raccoon: What's a henna-do?
Second raccoon: It runs around and says,
"Cluck, cluck!"

First raccoon: Have you given the goldfish
fresh water today?
Second raccoon: No. He didn't drink what I
gave him yesterday.

14

Weighty Walrus

What's brown, weighs two tons, and jumps higher than a house?

A walrus! Houses can't jump.

Why do walrus have only flippers?

Because they don't make tennis shoes for walrus.

What's white on the outside, brown in the middle, and heavy in your stomach?

A walrus sandwich.

What's red, weighs two tons, and sits in a
    cherry tree?
A walrus disguised as a cherry.

Why are walrus bad dancers?
'Cause they have two left flippers.

When the biggest walrus in the world fell into
    a 30-foot well, how did they get it out?
Wet.

Why is a walrus brown?
So you won't mistake him for a bluebird.

What do you get when you cross a parrot with
    a walrus?
A two-ton bird that eats peanuts.

What is the difference between a walrus and
    a blueberry?
A blueberry is blue.

What do you get if you cross a canary and a
walrus?

A pretty messy cage.

What would you get if you crossed a skunk
and a walrus?

A dirty look from the walrus.

How do you make a pickle laugh?

Tell it a walrus joke.

15

Amazing Animal Facts

Scientists estimate that there are over a
million kinds of animals on the earth. That
includes:

more than 800,000 kinds of insects.

more than 30,000 kinds of fish.

more than 9,000 kinds of insects.

more than 6,000 kinds of reptiles.

more than 3,000 kinds of amphibians.

more than 5,000 kinds of mammals.

The ears of the African elephant can grow as
large as four feet.

The eyes of the horse and ostrich are about 1 1/2 times larger than a human's eyes.

A chameleon's tongue is as long as its body.

Chameleons can change colors. They can also develop streaks and spots.

The kick from a cassowary bird from Australia can kill a man.

The coconut crab climbs trees, knocks down coconuts, breaks them open with its claws, and eats the coconut inside.

The flying dragon lizard is from the East Indies and Asia. It flies through the air from tree to tree on folds of skin that act like wings.

The duckbill platypus is mixed up. It has a bill like a duck, lays eggs like a bird, and has fur. It feeds its young like dogs do—with milk. The platypus lives in Tasmania and Australia.

A giant tortoise can live as long as 100 years.

The Napalese Swift is one type of bird that can fly as high as 20,000 feet—almost 4 miles above the earth!

Lemmings, small, short-tailed furry-footed rodents, migrate. Sometimes their path takes them into the sea—where many plunge in and drown.

The arctic tern flies a round-trip of about 22,000 miles when they migrate.

A camel can go several days without water, and it keeps a food supply of fat in its hump.

The kangaroo rat lives its lifetime without drinking water. It gets its water from the seeds it eats.

Lizards and snakes smell with their tongues.

Catfish are believed to have taste buds in their skin.

The average dog has the intelligence of a 3- to 4-year old child.

Gorillas pound their chests to scare away other gorillas.

Pinkish Duroc pigs have pink hair.

The average one-acre field will have 1.25 million spiders living on it.

Dogs sweat through their tongues.

A flea can jump as high as 12 inches.

The heart of a shrew beats close to 1,000
times per minute.

16

Crafty Crocodiles

How do crocodiles earn extra money?

They babysit for bluebirds on Saturday nights!

How do you know when a crocodile is going to charge?

When he shows his credit card.

How do you get down from a crocodile?

You don't. You get down from a goose.

Why did the crocodile walk around in polka-
dot socks?

Someone stole his sneakers.

How do you make a statue of a crocodile?

*Take a block of stone and carve away
everything that doesn't look like a crocodile.*

How do you make two crocodiles float?

*Put them on top of two scoops of ice cream in
a big glass of rootbeer.*

What's green on the inside and red and white
on the outside?

Campbell's Cream of Crocodile Soup.

What's a hitchhiking crocodile called?

Stranded.

What do you do when a crocodile sits on your hanky?

Wait for him to get up.

How do you know when there's a crocodile in your custard?

When it's lumpy—and the lumps move!

How do you get a crocodile in a Volkswagen bug?

Throw one of the dinosaurs out.

What would happen if a crocodile sat in front of you in class?

You'd have a hard time seeing the blackboard.

What's big and red and hides its face in the corner?

An embarrassed crocodile.

Why do crocodiles wear sandals?
To keep their feet from sinking in the sand.

How do you get a crocodile into a matchbox?
Take out the matches first.

Why do crocodiles have red eyes?
So they can hide in cherry trees.

17

Monkeyshines

First monkey: How can you get a set of teeth put in for free?

Second monkey: I have no clue.

First monkey: Kick a Saber Tooth Tiger.

First monkey: Where do young cows go to dance?

Second monkey: I can't guess.

First monkey: To the discowteque.

First monkey: When do pigs give their girlfriends presents?

Second monkey: I have no idea.
First monkey: On Valenswine's Day.

First monkey: What is a sick crocodile?
Second monkey: You tell me.
First monkey: An illigator.

First monkey: What do you get if you cross a
shark with a parrot?
Second monkey: Who knows?
First monkey: An animal that talks your ear
off.

First monkey: I wish I had enough money to
buy a walrus.
Second monkey: Why on earth do you want a
walrus?
First monkey: I don't. I just want the money.

First monkey: Did you hear about the rabbit
with the lisp who went to the dentist to get
his tooth extracted?

Second monkey: No, what happened?

First monkey: The dentist asked him if he wanted gas, and the rabbit answered, "No, I'm an ether bunny."

First monkey: What is a musical fish?

Second monkey: My mind is a blank.

First monkey: A piano-tuna.

First monkey: What animal are you like when you take a bath?

Second monkey: That's a mystery.

First monkey: A little bear.

First monkey: What animal uses a nut-cracker?

Second monkey: I'm blank.

First monkey: A toothless squirrel.

First monkey: In what kind of home do the buffalo roam?

Second monkey: I don't have the foggiest.
First monkey: A dirty one.

First monkey: What do you call a sheep that hangs out with 40 thieves?
Second monkey: I'm in the dark.
First monkey: Ali Baa Baa.

First monkey: Why do birds fly south?
Second monkey: Search me.
First monkey: If they walked it would be winter by the time they got there.

First monkey: What do you get if you blow your hair dryer down a rabbit hole?
Second monkey: I pass.
First monkey: Hot-cross bunnies.

First monkey: Which skunk smells the worst?
Second monkey: How should I know?
First monkey: The one with the cheapest perfume.

18

Happy Hippos

What happens when you cross a hippo with a cow?

We don't know . . . but it eats a lot of grass with a big mouth and gets unhappy when you milk it.

How do you shoot a white hippopotamus?

You hold his nose until he turns blue, then you shoot him with a blue hippopotamus gun.

Would you rather be attacked by a
hippopotamus or a gorilla?

*I'd rather the hippopotamus attacked the
gorilla.*

Why is a hippo gray, large, and wrinkled?

*Because if he were small, white, and round, he
would be an aspirin.*

Why did the hippo paint his toenails different
colors?

So he could hide in a jellybean bag.

What time is it when a hippo sits on your car?

Time to get a new car.

What do you get if you cross a spider with a
hippo?

*Who knows? But when it crawls across your
ceiling the roof will collapse!*

What's the difference between a hippo and an orange?

They're different colors.

Why did the hippo stand on the marshmallow?

So he wouldn't fall into the cocoa.

How do you stop a hippo from sticking his head out of the backseat window of a car?

Make him sit up front.

What is the best way to cure a hippo who walks in his sleep?

Put tacks on the floor.

Why do hippos eat raw vegetables?

Because they don't know how to cook.

What does an electric hippo say?

Watts up, Doc?

Why did the hippo paint himself all different
   colors?
So he could hide in the crayon box.

What is gray and blue and very big?
A hippo holding its breath.

How can you tell a hippo from spaghetti?
The hippo doesn't slip off the end of your fork.

How do you make a hippo stew?
Keep him waiting for two hours.

19

Armadillo Knock-Knocks

First armadillo: Knock, knock.

Second armadillo: Who's there?

First armadillo: Watson.

Second armadillo: Watson who?

First armadillo: Nothing much—what's new
with you?

First armadillo: Knock, knock.

Second armadillo: Who's there?

First armadillo: Mecca.

Second armadillo: Mecca who?

First armadillo: Mecca me happy!

First armadillo: Knock, knock.

Second armadillo: Who's there?

First armadillo: Gladys.

Second armadillo: Gladys who?

First armadillo: Gladys my last knock, knock joke?

First armadillo: Knock, knock.

Second armadillo: Who's there?

First armadillo: Mae.

Second armadillo: Mae who?

First armadillo: Maebe I'll tell you and maybe I won't!

First armadillo: Knock, knock.

Second armadillo: Who's there?

First armadillo: Abbott.

Second armadillo: Abbott who?

First armadillo: Abbott time you answered the door.

First armadillo: Knock, knock.

Second armadillo: Who's there?

First armadillo: Jilly.

Second armadillo: Jilly who?

First armadillo: Jilly out here, and I'm freezing. May I come in?

First armadillo: Knock, knock.

Second armadillo: Who's there?

First armadillo: Phyllis.

Second armadillo: Phyllis who?

First armadillo: Phyllis glass up with Coke, please. I'm thirsty!

First armadillo: Knock, knock.

Second armadillo: Who's there?

First armadillo: Emma.

Second armadillo: Emma who?

First armadillo: Emma tired, are you tired too?

First armadillo: Knock, knock.

Second armadillo: Who's there?

First armadillo: Mariet.

Second armadillo: Mariet who?

First armadillo: Mariet the whole bowl of popcorn.

First armadillo: Knock, knock.

Second armadillo: Who's there?

First armadillo: Paula.

Second armadillo: Paula who?

First armadillo: Paula the handle; the door is
open.

First armadillo: Knock, knock.

Second armadillo: Who's there?

First armadillo: Denise.

Second armadillo: Denise who?

First armadillo: Denise are connected to your
legs.

First armadillo: Knock, knock.

Second armadillo: Who's there?

First armadillo: Sue.

Second armadillo: Sue who?

First armadillo: Sue whomever you want. I didn't break your doorbell.

First armadillo: Knock, knock.
Second armadillo: Who's there?
First armadillo: Joan.
Second armadillo: Joan who?
First armadillo: Joan't you know who is knocking?

First armadillo: Knock, knock.
Second armadillo: Who's there?
First armadillo: Ida.
Second armadillo: Ida who?
First armadillo: Ida want to stand outside all night!

First armadillo: Knock, knock.
Second armadillo: Who's there?
First armadillo: Lily.
Second armadillo: Lily who?
First armadillo: Lily house on the prairie!

First armadillo: Knock, knock.

Second armadillo: Who's there?

First armadillo: Shirley.

Second armadillo: Shirley who?

First armadillo: Shirley you're going to open the door.

First armadillo: Knock, knock.

Second armadillo: Who's there?

First armadillo: Carrie.

Second armadillo: Carrie who?

First armadillo: Carrie me back to bed. I'm tired.

First armadillo: Knock, knock.

Second armadillo: Who's there?

First armadillo: Verdi.

Second armadillo: Verdi who?

First armadillo: Verdi been all day?

First armadillo: Knock, knock.
Second armadillo: Who's there?
First armadillo: Chopin.
Second armadillo: Chopin who?
First armadillo: Chopin the supermarket!

First armadillo: Knock, knock.
Second armadillo: Who's there?
First armadillo: Albee.
Second armadillo: Albee who?
First armadillo: Albee a monkey's uncle!

First armadillo: Knock, knock.
Second armadillo: Who's there?
First armadillo: Gable.
Second armadillo: Gable who?
First armadillo: Gable to leap tall buildings in
   a single bound!

First armadillo: Knock, Knock
Second armadillo: Who's there?
First armadillo: Amos.
Second armadillo: Amos who?
First armadillo: Amosquito just bit me.

First armadillo: Knock, Knock.
Second armadillo: Who's there?
First armadillo: Andy.
Second armadillo: Andy who?
First armadillo: Andy bit me again.

First armadillo: Knock, Knock.
Second armadillo: Who's there?
First armadillo: Oliver.
Second armadillo: Oliver who?
First armadillo: Oliver my body the mosquitoes are biting me.

First armadillo: Knock, Knock.
Second armadillo: Who's there?
First armadillo: Sarah.
Second armadillo: Sarah who.
First armadillo: Sarah a doctor that can stop all this itching?

20

The Camel's Collection

What is the main ingredient of dog biscuits?
Collieflour.

What kind of dog can fly?
A bird dog.

What do you get if you cross a kitten with a
  post?
A caterpillar.

What happened to the cat who swallowed a
ball of yarn?

She had mittens.

What happened to the cat who swallowed the
duck?

She became a duck-filled fatty-puss.

What is the difference between a cat and a
frog?

*A cat has nine lives, but a frog croaks every
night.*

What was the first cat to fly?

Kittyhawk

What happened to the dog that ate only garlic
and onions?

His bark was worse than his bite.

What do you call a meeting among many
    dogs?

A bow-wow pow-wow.

What do dogs always take on their camping
    trips?

Pup tents.

What would you get if you crossed a puppy
    with a mean boy?

A bullydog.

What would you get if you crossed a bear and
    a skunk?

Winnie-the-Phew.

What would you get if you crossed a pit bull
    and a cow?

An animal that's too mean to milk.

What would you get if you crossed a cat and a
   pair of galoshes?

Puss 'n' boots.

In what month do dogs bark the least?

February—it's the shortest month.

What would happen if everyone in the
   country owned a horse?

The country would be more stabilized.

What are the chickens doing out in front of
   your house?

*They heard some men were going to lay a
   sidewalk, and they wanted to see how it was
   done.*

What would you get if you crossed a parrot
   and a hyena?

*An animal that could tell you what it was
   laughing about.*

What do they do with old bowling balls?
They give them to elephants to use as marbles.

Which side of a chicken has the most
  feathers?
The outside.

Why do bees have sticky hair?
Because they use honeycombs.

21

Woolly Mammoths

What words do you use to scold a woolly
mammoth?

Tusk! Tusk!

Why does a woolly mammoth have a trunk?

*Because he'd look pretty silly with a glove
compartment.*

Which takes longer to get ready for a trip—a
rooster or a woolly mammoth?

*The woolly mammoth. He has to take a trunk,
while the rooster takes only his comb.*

What has two tails, six feet, and two trunks.

A woolly mammoth with spare parts.

What prehistoric animal spent most of its
time talking?

The woolly mammouth.

How can you tell if there is a woolly
mammoth in your sleeping bag?

By the smell of peanuts on his breath.

Why wasn't the woolly mammoth allowed on
the plane?

Because his trunk wouldn't fit under the seat.

Why do woolly mammoths' tusks stick out?
Because their parents couldn't afford braces.

Why do woolly mammoths have squinting
eyes?
*From reading the small print on peanut
packages!*

Why are woolly mammoths tusks easier to get
in Alabama?
Because their "Tuscaloosa."

Why does a woolly mammoth have a trunk?
To hide in when he sees a mouse!

Why do woolly mammoths have white tusks?
They use toothpaste!

Why do woolly mammoths have trunks?
*Because they don't have pockets to put things
in.*

Why do woolly mammoths carry keys?
To open their trunks.

How can you tell there's a woolly mammoth
  on your back during a storm?
You can hear his ears flapping in the breeze.

Why do woolly mammoths have trunks?
They'd look silly with suitcases, wouldn't they?

22

Dining with the Dingos

Dingo: Waiter, why does my tea have a fly in it?

Waiter: For a cup of tea that costs 60 cents, what do you expect—a dinosaur?

Dingo: Waiter, there's a fly in my stew.

Waiter: They don't care what they eat, do they?

Dingo: Waiter! What's this fly doing in my alphabet soup?

Waiter: Learning to read, sir!

Dingo: Waiter! There's a fly in my chow mein!
Waiter: That's nothing. Wait till you see
    what's in your fortune cookie.

Waiter: And what would you like, sir?
Dingo: I would like a crocodile sandwich,
    please, and make it snappy!

Dingo: Have you any wild duck?
Waiter: No, sir, but we can take a tame one
    and irritate him for you.

Dingo: Waiter, there's a bee in my soup!
Waiter: Yes, sir, it's the fly's day off.

Dingo: Waiter, what's this fly doing in my ice
    cream?
Waiter: Looks like it's learning to ski.

Waiter: Sir, we are famous for snails here.

Dingo: I thought so. I've been served by one
  already.

Dingo: Waiter, have you ever been to the zoo?

Waiter: No, sir.

Dingo: Well, you ought to go. You'd enjoy
  seeing the turtles whizzing by.

Dingo: Are you the lad who took my order?

Waiter: Yes, sir.

Dingo: My how you've grown!

Dingo: Waiter, there's a piece of canvas in my
  fish.

Waiter: Why not? It's a sailfish.

Dingo: Take back this steak. I've been trying
  to cut it for ten minutes, but it's so tough I
  can't make a dent in it.

Waiter: I'm sorry, sir, but I can't take it back.
  You've bent it.

23

Animal Quiz

How do bees make money?
They cell their honey!

How do robins get in shape?
They do worm-ups.

Who gets paid for never doing a day's work?
A night watchman.

Is writing on an empty stomach harmful?
No, but paper is better.

101

What do you call a rabbit who has never been out of the house?
An ingrown hare.

What well-known animal drives all over the road?
A road hog.

When does a caterpillar improve its morals?
When it turns over a new leaf.

What should a man know before trying to teach a dog?
More than the dog.

Imagine you were in the jungle and were being chased by a woolly mammoth. What would you do?
I would stop imagining!

How do you get a woolly mammoth out of a bathtub?
Pull the plug.

What's the highest form of animal life?
The giraffe.

Why did the grumpy man order chicken for
dinner?
He was in a fowl mood.

Why was the little mosquito up so late?
He had to study for his blood test!

How can you tell which end of a worm is its
head?
Tell it a joke and see which end laughs.

What do you get from petting rabbits with
sharp teeth?
Hare cuts.

What do you call a boy who sticks his right
arm down a lion's throat?
Lefty.

What do you get when you cross a tiger and a
parrot?

*I don't know, but when it asks for a cracker,
you'd better give it one!*

Why did the farmer wash the chicken's mouth
out with soap?

It was using fowl language.

What's gray, weighs 5 tons, and wears glass
slippers?

Cinderelephant.

What would you call a prehistoric skunk?

Exstink.

How do you treat a pig with a sore throat?

Apply oinkment.

What do you call a camel without a hump?

Humphrey.

What extra job did the snake do on rainy days?

He worked as a windshield viper.

What would you get if you crossed a flea with a rabbit?

A bug's bunny.

Which is less intelligent—a large chicken or a small chicken?

The large one is the bigger cluck.

What is the best way to hold a bat?

By the wings.

What is a ringleader?

The first pig in the bathtub.

What do you get when you cross a chicken with a construction worker?

A bricklayer.

Why is a pig in the house like a house afire?
Because the sooner you put it out, the better.

What did Hannibal get when he crossed the
  Alps with elephants?
Mountains that never forget.

What is yellow, smooth, and very dangerous?
Shark-infested custard.

What did the dinosaur think of the grape's
  house?
Devine.

If a dinosaur were eating your book, what
  would you do?
I would take the words right out of his mouth.

What's green and stamps out jungle fires?
Smoky the dinosaur.

How can you tell if there is a dinosaur in the
   refrigerator?
The door won't shut.

How do you lift a dinosaur?
Put him on an acorn and let it grow.

Names for Baby Animals

Animal name	Baby name
Albatross	fledgling
Beaver	kit
Cat	kitten
Deer	fawn
Donkey	foal
Giraffe	calf
Goose	gosling
Hog	shoat
Kangaroo	joey
Ostrich	chick
Rabbit	kit
Seal	pup
Sheep	lamb
Swan	cygnet
Turkey	poult
Zebra	colt

Dizzy Dinosaurs

What do you call a dinosaur hitchhiker?

A ten-and-a-half-ton pickup.

What do you call a dinosaur who's always
    walking in mud?

Browntoesaurus.

Who was the scariest dinosaur of them all?

The terrordactyl.

What kind of dinosaurs live in graveyards?
Cemeterydactyls.

What's big and fierce and worn around your
  neck?
A tierannosaurus.

What do you call a dinosaur that steps on
  everything in its way?
Tyrannosaurus Wrecks.

What do you call a dinosaur in a hurry?
A prontosaurus.

Why do ducks have webbed feet?
To stamp out forest fires.

Why do dinosaurs have flat feet?
To stamp out burning ducks!

What kind of eggs does a wicked dinosaur lay?

Deviled eggs.

What do you call a prehistoric animal the day after it's exercised much too much?

A Dinosore.

26

Animal Tales

While taking a long drink at a pond, a dinosaur happened to glance up and spotted a snapping turtle lying on a nearby stone. Its eyes narrowing, the dinosaur lumbered over, raised a foot, and pressed the turtle flat.

Observing the murder from the jungle, a zebra wandered over.

"Why did you do that?" he asked.

"This was the same animal that bit off the tip of my nose over ten years ago."

"The zebra's eyes widened. "The same one? You must have an incredible memory!"

Raising its head proudly, the dinosaur said, "Turtle recall."

Recipe for Dinosaur Stew

One dinosaur, two rabbits (optional), brown gravy, salt, and pepper. Cut the dinosaur into small bite-size pieces. This should take about two months. Add enough brown gravy to cover. Cook over kerosene stove for about four weeks at 464 degrees. This will serve 3,800 people. If more are expected, two rabbits may be added, but do this only if necessary—most people don't like to find hares in their stew.

Deep in the jungle, a trio of animals were discussing who among them was the most powerful.

"I am," said the hawk, "because I can fly and swoop down swiftly at my prey."

"I am," said the mountain lion, "because I am not only fleet, but I have powerful teeth and claws."

"I am," said the skunk, "because with a flick of my tail, I can drive off the two of you."

Suddenly a huge dinosaur lumbered over and settled the debate by eating them all, hawk, lion, and stinker.

Mama Gnu was waiting for Papa Gnu when he came home for dinner one evening.

"Our little boy was very bad today," she declared. "I want you to punish him."

"Oh no", said Papa Gnu. "I won't punish him. You'll have to learn to paddle your own gnu."

A gorilla walked into a drugstore and ordered a 50-cent sundae. He put down a ten-dollar bill to pay for it. The clerk thought, "What can a gorilla know about money?" So he handed back a single dollar in change.

As he did, he said, "You know, we don't get many gorillas in here."

"No wonder," answered the gorilla, "at nine dollars a sundae."

For many years a certain white whale and a tiny herring had been inseparable friends. Wherever the white whale roamed in search of food, the herring was sure to be swimming right along beside him.

One fine spring day the herring turned up off the coast of Norway without his companion. Naturally all the other fish were curious, and an octopus finally asked the herring what happened to his friend the whale.

"How should I know?" the herring replied. "Am I my blubber's kipper?"

27

Cockroach Comedy

What is a mosquito's favorite sport?
Skin diving.

How do you start a firefly race?
On your mark, get set, glow.

Which ant is an army officer?
Sergeant.

What goes tick-tock croak, tick-tock croak?
A watch frog.

Which bug gobbles up trash?
The litterbug.

What famous baseball player drives bugs
batty?
Mickey Mantis.

Why did the grasshopper go to the doctor?
Because he felt jumpy.

28

Wild Whales

How can you tell when there is a whale under your bed?

When you are nearly touching the ceiling.

What do you get when you cross a Saber Tooth Tiger with a whale?

A very nervous mailman.

What's the best way to raise a whale?

Use a crane.

Why do whales paint their flippers all
different colors?

So they can hide in jellybean jars.

But I've never seen a whale in a jellybean jar.

See how good they hide!

Why do whales lie down?

Because they can't lie up.

What's blue and lumpy and comes in a can?

Cream of Whale Soup.

Which whales don't get cavities?

Those that use toothpaste.

If 20 whales swam after 1 fisherman, what
time is it?

Twenty after one.

What was the whale doing on the road?
Trying to trip the ants with its flipper.

Why did the whale cross the road?
To prove he wasn't chicken.

How do you make a whale sandwich?
First of all you get a very large loaf of bread . .

What's as big as a whale and doesn't weigh anything?
A whale's shadow.

Why did the whale lie in the road with his flippers in the air?
He wanted to trip the birds.

Why did the whale sit on a red cherry?
So his flipper wouldn't get into the chocolate sundae.

If a whale was on a leaf in a tree, how would
it get down?
*It would wait for autumn, then float down
with the leaf.*

How do you make a slow whale fast?
Don't feed him!

What's the difference between a girl whale
and a boy whale?
One sings soprano, one sings bass.

Why do whales never lie?
The ground isn't very comfortable.

What's blue and red all over?
A sunburned whale.

29

Mickey Moose

What do you get if you cross a moose with a
boy scout?

A moose that helps old ladies cross the street.

What is the best thing to take when you're
run over by a moose?

*The license plate number of the car the moose
was driving.*

What did the moose say when it was put into the pot on the stove?

Boy am I in hot water!

Why do moose wear sneakers while jumping from tree to tree?

So they don't get splinters!

Why do moose wear sunglasses?

So Tarzan won't recognize them!

What did the moose say when he saw Frenchman Charles de Gaulle?

Nothing . . . he couldn't speak French!

What would you get if Batman and Robin were run over by a herd of stampeding moose?

Flatman and Ribbon.

When does a mouse weigh as much as a
  moose?
When the scale is broken.

If you were on the great plains by yourself
  and a moose charged you, what would you
  do?
Pay him.

If there were three moose in a kitchen, which
  one would be a cowboy?
The one on the range.

What's the difference between a moose and an
  orange?
One hangs on a tree and doesn't have antlers.

How do you lift a moose?
Put him on a flower and let it grow.

Why did the moose wear sunglasses?
*With all the silly moose riddles around, he
  didn't want to be recognized.*

30

Ostrich Knock-Knocks

First ostrich: Knock, knock.

Second ostrich: Who's there?

First ostrich: Donna

Second ostrich: Donna who?

First ostrich: Donna keep me waiting
out here.

First ostrich: Knock, knock.

Second ostrich: Who's there?

First ostrich: Wendy.

Second ostrich: Wendy who?

First ostrich: Wendy door opens, I'll come in.

First ostrich: Knock, knock.
Second ostrich: Who's there?
First ostrich: Elsie.
Second ostrich: Elsie who?
First ostrich: Elsie you in my dreams.

First ostrich: Knock, knock.
Second ostrich: Who's there?
First ostrich: Celeste.
Second ostrich: Celeste who?
First ostrich: Celeste time I knock on this
    door!

First ostrich: Knock, knock.
Second ostrich: Who's there?
First ostrich: Doris.
Second ostrich: Doris who?
First ostrich: Doris shut, that's why I'm
    knocking.

First ostrich: Knock, knock.
Second ostrich: Who's there?
First ostrich: Yura.
Second ostrich: Yura who?
First ostrich: Yura great friend.

First ostrich: Knock, knock.
Second ostrich: Who's there?
First ostrich: Carrot.
Second ostrich: Carrot who?
First ostrich: Carrot me back to old Virginia.

First ostrich: Knock, knock.
Second ostrich: Who's there?
First ostrich: Castro.
Second ostrich: Castro who?
First ostrich: Castro bread upon the waters.

First ostrich: Knock, knock.
Second ostrich: Who's there?
First ostrich: Toby.
Second ostrich: Toby who?
First ostrich: Toby or not Toby, that is the
    question . . .

First ostrich: Knock, knock.
Second ostrich: Who's there?
First ostrich: Iris.
Second ostrich: Iris who?
First ostrich: Iris I was rich!

First ostrich: Knock, knock.
Second ostrich: Who's there?
First ostrich: Costa.
Second ostrich: Costa who?
First ostrich: Costa lot.

First ostrich: Knock, knock.
Second ostrich: Who's there?
First ostrich: Iran.
Second ostrich: Iran who?
First ostrich: Iran over to see you.

First ostrich: Knock, knock.
Second ostrich: Who's there?
First ostrich: Jess.
Second ostrich: Jess who?
First ostrich: Jess a friend of yours.

First ostrich: Knock, knock.
Second ostrich: Who's there?
First ostrich: Missouri.

Second ostrich: Missouri who?
First ostrich: Missouri loves company!

First ostrich: Knock, knock.
Second ostrich: Who's there?
First ostrich: Gravy.
Second ostrich: Gravy who?
First ostrich: Gravy Crockett.

First ostrich: Knock, knock.
Second ostrich: Who's there?
First ostrich: Halibut.
Second ostrich: Halibut who?
First ostrich: Halibut a kiss, sweetie?

First ostrich: Knock, knock.
Second ostrich: Who's there?
First ostrich: Congo.
Second ostrich: Congo who?
First ostrich: Congo out, I'm grounded.

First ostrich: Knock, knock.
Second ostrich: Who's there?
First ostrich: Egypt.
Second ostrich: Egypt who?
First ostrich: Egypt me out of money.

First ostrich: Knock, knock.
Second ostrich: Who's there?
First ostrich: Iowa.
Second ostrich: Iowa who?
First ostrich: Iowa you a dollar.

First ostrich: Knock, knock.
Second ostrich: Who's there?
First ostrich: Havana.
Second ostrich: Havana who?
First ostrich: Havana good time?

First ostrich: Knock, knock.
Second ostrich: Who's there?
First ostrich: Yukon.
Second ostrich: Yukon who?
First ostrich: Yukon let me in now.

First ostrich: Knock, knock.
Second ostrich: Who's there?
First ostrich: Sam.
Second ostrich: Sam who?
First ostrich: Samday my prince will come.

First ostrich: Knock, knock.
Second ostrich: Who's there?
First ostrich: Woody.
Second ostrich: Woody who?
First ostrich: Woody open the door, please?

31

Berserk Buffalo

What does a buffalo become after it is 49 years old?

Fifty years old.

Is it true that a buffalo won't attack you if you carry a flashlight?

That depends on how fast you carry it.

What is brown and has 16 wheels?

A buffalo on roller skates.

How do you run over a buffalo?
Climb up its tail, dash to its head, and slide down its nose.

What's brown and shaggy, weighs ten tons, and plays squash?
A buffalo in a phone booth.

What did one buffalo say to the other?
Nothing! Buffalo can't talk—they only whistle.

Why do buffalo have sore ankles?
From wearing their sneakers too tight!

Why do buffalo wear blue sneakers?
Their yellow ones aren't in style!

How does a buffalo get in a tree?
He hides in an acorn and waits for a squirrel to carry him up!

Why do girl buffalo wear angora sweaters?
To tell them apart from boy buffalo!

What is the most dangerous thing for buffalo
to do when they are visiting the city?
Get their tails caught in subway doors!

Why do buffalo live on the great plains?
It's away from the high-rent district!

Why do buffalo climb up palm trees?
To try out their new sneakers!

Why don't buffalo go to college?
They don't fit through the door!

Animal Feet

Cows have split hooves.

Seals have flippers.

Lions have paws.

Frogs have webbed feet.

Elephants have single-member feet.

Sloths have claws.

Geckos have adhesive pads.

Horses have singled-toed hooves.

Bashful Bears

Why do bears wear short shorts?

You'd sweat too, if you wore long pants in the forest heat!

How do you catch a bear?

First you take a pair of tweezers, binoculars, a milk carton, and a sign that has "Bear" spelled wrong. Then you take the sign into a forest, hang it from a tree and wait for a bear to come along and correct the spelling. While he's figuring out how to do it, you look at him through the wrong end of the binoculars, pick him up with the tweezers, and put him in the milk carton.

What's the difference between a bear and
peanut butter?
A bear won't stick to the roof of your mouth.

How do you get a bear into a telephone booth?
Open the door.

Why can't a bear ride a bicycle?
Because he has no thumbs to ring the bell.

What did the bear say to the platypus?
*I never forget a face, but with yours I'll make
an exception.*

What can you say about nine bears wearing
pink sneakers and one bear wearing blue?
Nine out of ten bears wear pink sneakers.

Why did the bear paint himself all different
colors?
So he could hide in a package of M&Ms.

How do you stop a bear passing through the eye of a needle?

Tie a knot in his tail.

What did the grape say when the bear stepped on it?

Nothing, it just let out a little whine.

How do you get a bear into a popcorn box?

You don't. They only come in Crackerjacks.

34

Dashing Dinosaurs

What's gray and comes in ten-gallon jars?
Instant dinosaurs.

Why did the dinosaur sit on the tomato?
He wanted to play squash.

When is a dinosaur most likely to enter your house?
When the door is open.

What's green on the inside and clear on the outside?
A dinosaur in a plastic bag.

What color hair tint does a dinosaur use?
*How should I know? Only her hairdresser
knows for sure.*

What was the dinosaur doing on the road?
About two miles an hour.

Why did the dinosaur wear green sneakers?
His blue ones were at the laundry.

What's gray, weighs ten tons, and flies?
A dinosaur in a helicopter.

What's red, blue, white, and orange?
A plaid dinosaur.

How do you know when there's a dinosaur in
your bed?
He has a "D" on his pajamas.

What's the best way to get something out
from under a dinosaur?

Wait for the dinosaur to go away.

What did the dinosaur say when the monkey
stepped on his foot?

*With tears in his eyes he said, "Why don't you
pick on someone your own size?"*

Why did the dinosaur sit on a tack?

To see how high he could jump.

Who started the dinosaur jokes?

That's what the dinosaurs would like to know!

Did you hear about the man that shot a
dinosaur in his pajamas?

How did the dinosaur get into his pajamas?

Why do dinosaurs step on lily pads?

Because the water won't hold them up.

Why do dinosaurs clip their toenails?
So their ballet slippers will fit.

What's green and lights up?
An electric dinosaur.

What do you do when a dinosaur stubs his toe?
Call a very big toe truck.

What did the plant-eating dinosaur say when winter ended and the trees sprouted new growth?
Whew! That's a releaf!

What weighs ten tons, has a long neck, and cuts through wood?
A dinosaw.

35

Amusing Anteater Antics

First anteater: Why shouldn't you cry when a cow falls on the ice?
Second anteater: Beats me.
First anteater: Because it is no use crying over spilled milk.

First anteater: What is the name of your dog?
Second anteater: Ginger.
First anteater: Does Ginger bite?
Second anteater: No, Ginger snaps!

First anteater: Why can't you talk with a goat around?
Second anteater: I can't guess.
First anteater: He's always butting in.

First anteater: The woolly mammoth was arrested for stealing a pig.

Second anteater: How did they prove it?

First anteater: The pig squealed.

First anteater: What do you call a donkey who carries a man?

Second anteater: I have no idea.

First anteater: A hee-hawler.

First anteater: What's black and white and red all over?

Second anteater: You tell me.

First anteater: A sunburned zebra.

First anteater: What's white outside, green inside, and hops?

Second anteater: I give up.

First anteater: A frog sandwich.

First anteater: Name six things smaller than an ant's mouth.

Second anteater: I can't.

First anteater: Six of his teeth.

First anteater: Why was the insect kicked out of the national park?

Second anteater: You've got me.

First anteater: Because it was a litterbug.

First anteater: How does a nut feel when a squirrel chews on it?

Second anteater: My mind is a blank.

First anteater: Nut so good.

First anteater: What do you get if you cross a skunk and a boomerang?

Second anteater: That's a mystery.

First anteater: A smell you can't get rid of.

First anteater: If my cat won an Oscar, what would he get?

Second anteater: I'm blank.
First anteater: The acatemy award.

First anteater: What animal doesn't play fair?
Second anteater: I don't have the foggiest.
First anteater: A cheetah.

First anteater: How does an octopus go into battle?
Second anteater: It's unknown to me.
First anteater: Well armed.

First anteater: Why did the city rat gnaw a hole in the carpet?
Second anteater: Search me.
First anteater: Because he wanted to see the floor show.

First anteater: Did you hear about the horse who ate an electric wire instead of hay?
Second anteater: You've got me guessing.
First anteater: He went haywire.

First anteater: What's black and white and red all over?

Second anteater: I pass.

First anteater: A sunburned penguin.

First anteater: What kind of story is the story about the three little pigs?

Second anteater: How should I know.

First anteater: A pigtail.

36

Elephant Entertainment

What's gray and lumpy and comes in a can?
Cream of Elephant Soup.

Why do elephants have toenails?
So they can have something to chew!

What's pink, slimy, and weighs 5 tons?
An inside-out elephant.

What's red, weighs 5 tons, and sits in a cherry tree?
An elephant disguised as a cherry.

What goes "Clomp, clomp, clomp, swish-
clomp, clomp, clomp, clomp, swish-clomp?"
An elephant with one wet tennis shoe.

Who started elephant jokes?
That's what the elephant wants to know!

Why are elephants bad dancers?
'Cause they have two left feet.

Why is an elephant gray?
So you won't mistake him for a bluebird.

What do you get when you cross a parrot with
an elephant?
A five-ton bird that eats peanuts.

What is the difference between an elephant
and a blueberry?
A blueberry is blue.

What do you get if you cross a canary and an
elephant?
A pretty messy cage.

How do you make a pickle laugh?
Tell it an elephant joke.

37

Dainty Dolphins

How do dolphins dive into swimming pools?

Head first.

If you catch a white dolphin with a white fishing pole, what do you catch a pink dolphin with?

No, not a pink fishing pole. You paint the dolphin white then catch it with a white fishing pole.

Why can't dolphins fly?
They don't have propellers.

Why did the dolphin paint her head yellow?
She wanted to see if blondes have more fun.

Why do dolphins have wrinkles?
Have you ever tried to iron one?

How do you get a dolphin out of a Jell-O box?
Read the directions on the back.

How do you get a dolphin out of a can?
Get a can opener.

How do you know when there's a dolphin in
the refrigerator?
*You can see his flipper marks in the
cheesecake.*

What is green and hangs on a tree?
An unripe dolphin.

What did the psychiatrist say to the dolphin?
That'll be 30 dollars for the visit . . . and 300 to help dry out the couch.

Does your dolphin bite strangers?
Only when he doesn't know them.

Why did the dolphin swim on his back?
So he wouldn't get his tennis shoes wet.

38

Yak Yuk-Yuks

First yak: Why was the dolphin so sad?
Second yak: It had no porpoise in life.

First yak: What do you call the author of a western story?
Second yak: A horseback writer.

First yak: How does a fish pay his bills.
Second yak: With a credit cod.

First yak: What do you call a bug that hates Christmas?
Second yak: A humbug!

First yak: What do you call a rabbit with fleas?

Second yak: Bugs Bunny!

First yak: If you were walking alongside a donkey, what fruit would you represent?

Second yak: A pear.

First yak: Where do salmon go to sleep?

Second yak: On the riverbed.

First yak: How many monkeys can you put into an empty barrel?

Second yak: One. After that the barrel isn't empty.

First yak: Why do birds hang around libraries?

Second yak: To catch bookworms.

Rollicking Rhinos

What would happen if a rhinoceros swallowed a frog?

It might croak.

Is it difficult to bury a dead rhinoceros?

Yes, it's a huge undertaking.

What happened to Ray when he was stepped on by a rhinoceros?

He became an X-ray.

What do you do if a rhinoceros sneezes?
Get out of the way!

What weighs 10 tons, has a horn, and is
    bright red?
An embarrassed rhino.

How do you tell a rhino from a banana?
Try lifting it. If you can't get it off the floor, it's
    probably a rhino. But—it might be a heavy
    banana.

What hangs on a tree and shouts "Help!"?
A rhino in distress.

What's best for a blue rhino?
A trip to the circus to cheer him up.

What do you give a seasick rhino?
Plenty of room.

What was the rhino doing on the interstate?
About 10 miles per hour.

What's bright blue and weighs 5 tons?
A rhino holding its breath.

What did the apple say to the rhino?
Nothing. Apples can't talk.

What's gray, weighs five tons, and leaves
    footprints in the butter?
A rhino in the fridge.

What's a rhino in a fridge called?
A very tight squeeze.

What do rhino say when they bump into each
    other?
Small world, isn't it?

40

Hummingbird Humor

First hummingbird: Do fish perspire?

Second hummingbird: Naturally. What do you think makes the sea salty?

First hummingbird: Where is Moscow located?

Second hummingbird: In the barn with Pa's cow.

First hummingbird: Am I crazy if I talk to myself?

Second hummingbird: No, but you are if you pay attention.

41

Animal Hodgepodge

Did you hear about the two kangaroos? They lived hoppily ever after.

First squirrel: Did you know it takes three sheep to make one sweater?

Second squirrel: I didn't even know they could knit.

First spider: These mosquitoes are pretty pesky. Why don't you shoo them?

Second spider: It's too expensive. We just let them go barefoot.

First pig: A snake just snapped at me.
Second pig: Don't be silly. Snakes don't snap.
First pig: This one did. It was a garter snake.

Two boll weevils came from the country to the
city. One became rich and famous. The
other remained the lesser of the two
weevils.

Did you hear about the man who crossed a
parrot with a centipede . . . he got a walkie
talkie.

Did you hear about the man who crossed a
turkey with a centipede? On Thanksgiving,
everybody got a drumstick.

Did you hear about the man who crossed an
octopus with a bale of straw and got a
broom with eight handles?

Did you hear about the man who crossed a carrier pigeon with a woodpecker so when it delivers the message, it can knock on the door?

First chinchilla: Did you like the story about the dog who ran two miles just to pick up a stick?

Second chinchilla: No, I thought it was a little farfetched.

42

Zany Zoo Zingers

Whale: Why did the dolphins paint their flippers red?

Walrus: I don't know. Why?

Whale: So they could hide in the strawberry patch.

Whale: Did you ever see a dolphin in a strawberry patch?

Walrus: No!

Whale: That proves it works.

Sea lion: Is a dolphin big enough to eat when it's two weeks old?

Seal: Of course not.

Sea lion: Then how does it manage to live?

Cougar: Your sign says, "$50 to anyone who orders something we can't furnish." I would like to have a moose-ear sandwich.

Waiter: Ohhh . . . we're going to have to pay you the $50.

Cougar: No moose ears, huh?

Waiter: Oh, we've got lots of them . . . but we're all out of those big buns!

43

Hamster Humor

Fist hamster: What kind of bird always sounds cheerful?

Second hamster: A hummingbird.

First hamster: What is the most religious bird?

Second hamster: A bird of pray.

First hamster: What do you get when you cross a mustang with an elephant?

Second hamster: A sports car with plenty of trunk space.

First hamster: What do you get if you cross a kangaroo with a large jet?

Second hamster: A kangaroo that shows movies in its pouch.

First hamster: Why did the man bring a bag of feathers to the store?

Second hamster: He wanted to make a down payment.

First hamster: Why was the bird-lover carrying a bag of worms?

Second hamster: For a lark.

First hamster: Where do fireflies keep their cars?

Second hamster: In sparking lots.

First hamster: Is there a theory that some dinosaurs had feathers?

Second hamster: Yes, but it's for the birds.

First hamster: What is the difference between a chocolate-chip cookie and a whale?

Second hamster: Did you ever try dunking a whale in your milk?

First hamster: Where do cows go on vacation?

Second hamster: Moo York.

44

Goofy Geese

First goose: How do you catch a runaway dog?

Second goose: Hide behind a tree and make a noise like a bone.

First goose: Why is a dog so hot in the summer?

Second goose: Because it wears a coat and pants.

First goose: What is another name for a cat's home?

Second goose: A scratch pad.

First goose: What do you call a four-foot python?

Second goose: Shorty.

First goose: Should you ever eat a green snake?

Second goose: No! Wait until it ripens.

First goose: What holiday is strictly observed by all birds?

Second goose: Father's Day.

First goose: What does an eagle like to write with?

Second goose: A bald-point pen.

First goose: What kind of fish can you find in a birdcage?

Second goose: A perch.

First goose: What do you call a duck that
  likes to swim with alligators?
Second goose: Dinner.

First goose: What goes "zzub, zzub"?
Second goose: A bee flying backward.

First goose: Where do rabbits go when they
  get married?
Second goose: On their bunnymoon.

45

Wildcat Wisecracks

First wildcat: What do you get if you cross a
kangaroo and an elephant?

Second wildcat: Giant holes all over Australia.

First wildcat: What happened to the frog's car
when the parking meter expired?

Second wildcat: It got toad away.

First wildcat: What did the cowboy say when
his dog fell over the cliff?

Second wildcat: Dog-gone.

First wildcat: Where does a sheep get its hair cut?

Second wildcat: At the baa-baa shop.

First wildcat: What do you get if you cross a frog and a dog?

Second wildcat: A croaker spaniel.

First wildcat: What do you get when you cross a cow with a kangaroo?

Second wildcat: A kangamoo.

First wildcat: What do they call a duck who only gets A's on its report card?

Second wildcat: A wisequacker.

First wildcat: What kind of cows giggle?

Second wildcat: Laughingstock.

First wildcat: How do you know when it's raining cats and dogs?

Second wildcat: When you step on a poodle.

46

Monkey Mania

First monkey: What kind of fly has a frog in its throat?

Second monkey: A hoarsefly.

First monkey: What did the mole publish?

Second monkey: An underground newspaper.

First monkey: Did you hear about the dog that went to the flea circus?

Second monkey: No, what happened?

First monkey: He stole the show.

First monkey: Why do fish like to eat worms
so much?

Second monkey: I guess they're just hooked
on them.

First monkey: How do you start a flea
market?

Second monkey: From scratch.

First monkey: Why was the elephant annoyed
at his date?

Second monkey: She took too long to powder
her nose.

First monkey: How do you make a tarantula
shake?

Second monkey: Run up behind it and say,
"Boo!"

First monkey: What was Mrs. Chicken
reading?

Second monkey: An *Awesome Animal "Yolk"
Book for Kids.* It's a yolk . . . get it?

First monkey: How does a caterpillar start the day?

Second monkey: It turns over a new leaf.

First monkey: Where do horses stay when they're at a hotel?

Second monkey: In the bridle suite.

First monkey: What insect lives on next to nothing?

Second monkey: The moth—it always eats holes.

First monkey: How do you drive a herd of cattle?

Second monkey: Use a *steer*ing wheel.

Other Books by Bob Phillips

- The All-American Quote Book
- The All-New Clean Joke Book
- Anger Is a Choice
- Awesome Animal Jokes for Kids
- The Awesome Book of Bible Trivia
- Awesome Good Clean Jokes for Kids
- The Best of the Good Clean Jokes
- Bible Brainteasers
- Big Book—The Bible—Questions and Answers
- The Bible Olympics
- Bob Phillips' Encyclopedia of Good Clean Jokes
- Crazy Good Clean Jokes for Kids
- The Delicate Art of Dancing with Porcupines
- Friendship, Love & Laughter
- God's Hand over Hume
- Good Clean Jokes for Kids
- Goofy Good Clean Jokes for Kids
- The Great Bible Challenge
- The Handbook for Headache Relief
- How Can I Be Sure? A Pre-Marriage Inventory
- Humor Is Tremendous

- Loony Good Clean Jokes for Kids
- More Awesome Good Clean Jokes for Kids
- Nutty Good Clean Jokes for Kids
- Praise Is a Three-Lettered Word—Joy
- Redi-Reference
- Redi-Reference Daily Bible Reading Plan
- The Return of the Good Clean Jokes
- Tricks, Stunts, and Good Clean Fun
- Silly Stunts and Terrific Tricks for Kids
- Ultimate Good Clean Jokes for Kids
- The Unofficial Liberal Joke Book
- Wacky Good Clean Jokes for Kids
- What to Do Until the Psychiatrist Comes
- Wild & Wooly Clean Jokes for Kids
- Wit and Wisdom
- The World's Greatest Collection of Clean Jokes
- The World's Greatest Collection of Heavenly Humor

For information on how to purchase any of the above books, contact your local bookstore or send a self-addressed stamped envelope to:

Family Services
P.O. Box 9363
Fresno, CA 93702